01-15

the EVOLUTION *of*
TRAINING & COACHING

the EVOLUTION *of* TRAINING & COACHING

How to Explode Your Company Fast

SCOTT PALAT

New York

the EVOLUTION *of* TRAINING & COACHING
How to Explode Your Company Fast

Published in New York, New York, by Morgan James Publishing. Morgan James and The Entrepreneurial Publisher are trademarks of Morgan James, LLC.
www.MorganJamesPublishing.com

The Morgan James Speakers Group can bring authors to your live event. For more information or to book an event visit The Morgan James Speakers Group at www.TheMorganJamesSpeakersGroup.com.

A free eBook edition is available
with the purchase of this print book.

CLEARLY PRINT YOUR NAME ABOVE IN UPPER CASE

Instructions to claim your free eBook edition:
1. Download the BitLit app for Android or iOS
2. Write your name in **UPPER CASE** on the line
3. Use the BitLit app to submit a photo
4. Download your eBook to any device

ISBN 978-1-63047-246-7 paperback
ISBN 978-1-63047-247-4 eBook
ISBN 978-1-63047-248-1 hardcover
Library of Congress Control Number:
2014938442

Cover Design by:
Rachel Lopez
www.r2cdesign.com

Interior Design by:
Bonnie Bushman
bonnie@caboodlegraphics.com

In an effort to support local communities, raise awareness and funds, Morgan James Publishing donates a percentage of all book sales for the life of each book to Habitat for Humanity Peninsula and Greater Williamsburg.

Get involved today, visit
www.MorganJamesBuilds.com

TABLE OF CONTENTS

Intro for Coaches, Experts and Authors *vii*
Intro for Trainers and Managers *xi*

Chapter 1	My First Evolutionary Baby Step Started Here	1
Chapter 2	The Real Evolution Begins…	5
Chapter 3	The Evolution Continues…	8
Chapter 4	My Evolution Stopped Cold In Its Tracks	11
Chapter 5	It Felt Good To Evolve Again…	14
Chapter 6	Forced Evolution	18
Chapter 7	When Evolution Feels Right, Go For It…	25
Chapter 8	When Clients Request A More Personal Approach (And They Will), Evolve To Serve Them	29
Chapter 9	Stress Will Force Evolution Upon You	32
Chapter 10	Writing A Book Was NOT Good Enough— Evolution Forced Me To Ensure My Clients Achieved Success No Matter What	36

Chapter 11 I Evolved So Much That It Only Felt Right 40
 To Offer A *Power Guarantee* - A Money Back
 Guarantee On Making Money
Chapter 12 Evolution Full Circle 44
Chapter 13 Yet Another Evolutionary Twist 48
Chapter 14 Evolutionary Training & Coaching 55
 Software Was Released
Chapter 15 Evolution Made Me Re-Think Corporate 59
 Training. If Companies Can't Ensure Specific
 Results, Actions or Accountability, What
 Good Is Training At All?
Chapter 16 Evolve Your Job Training Programs Now 69
 Or All Heck Could Break Loose In Your
 Company
Chapter 17 It Takes Guts To Evolve This Way, 74
 But The Payoff Is Huge
Chapter 18 How To Take Evolutionary Action 79

Intro for Coaches, Experts and Authors

If you are already considered an expert in your field, but want to become the best you can be, and impact even more people than you already have, then this is the book for you! It will open your mind to a new way of thinking that revolves around promising your clients guaranteed results and creating a brand new source of high-ticket income you did not have before.

The evolution you are about to experience as you read this book will not happen until the end, but it's important for you to read each chapter so you can see how this hidden treasure was discovered, and why it has been out of your sight until now.

If you are like most experts, you probably have some or all of the following: books, DVD's, membership sites, courses, coaching programs, paid speaking engagements and more. As you have spread your knowledge throughout the

years, there is no doubt you had a tremendous impact on the lives of the people who found your information. For this, I congratulate you!

Now that we have established that you are indeed an expert, have you ever wondered how many of your customers and clients actually took action, using what you taught them? How many buy your books or courses and never get past the first chapter or lesson?

Of those same people, how many blame you for their lack of success?

If you never got blamed, consider yourself lucky! I've been blamed for my client's lack of success in the past and that is what forced me to evolve in such a way that I am now able to guarantee results for my clients.

Can you imagine being able to guarantee results for your clients?

If not, that's OK! This book was written to show you how to not only guarantee results, but also charge a premium for your service and have accountability steps in place so your clients can never place the blame on you.

If you are considered a high level coach and already guarantee results for your clients, kudos to you! Whether you guarantee overall success, or a specific percentage of increased revenue, chances are that you have to be intimate with your clients to help them achieve this level of success.

The only problem with this type of coaching from a business standpoint is that you are trading dollars for hours. If you ever wanted to change that, you would need a team of coaches you

can trust to have true leverage. From there, your coaches could help more people get results.

This new way of coaching that guarantees results does not have to be so time intensive. Of course if you just love coaching and are having fun helping your clients succeed, keep doing it and enjoy the ride.

If you want to discover a simpler way to take all of your other training materials and create a <u>brand new, high ticket product or service</u> that helps your clients achieve specific results while freeing up your time, you'll love this book!

This book will show you how to help more people in less time with your existing content. The best part is that you can present it in such a way that you can guarantee results while having accountability steps in place so you don't get blamed if your client does not take action and/or show you their work.

When you step back and take a look at all the success processes or methods you already have defined, I'll show you how each one of those can be a new source of income. Plus, you'll help more people achieve life-changing results NOW!

As a result of being so bold by guaranteeing a result, you will experience a demand unlike anything you have yet to see. The publicity and followers that will come from being able to offer a power guarantee will explode your company beyond what you thought was possible. This is my promise to you!

When it's all said and done, your clients will be grateful for your results focused, personalized, automated experience. This was part of my evolution and someday soon it's my hope that it will be a part of yours too.

INTRO FOR TRAINERS
AND MANAGERS

If you are a trainer or manager in charge of hiring and overseeing others within your company, this book will help you fine tune procedures, put accountability steps in place, and produce real results that not only justify the money you earn, but also make you feel compelled to ask for more.

Your company probably already has some form of procedures in place for new and existing employees. If by chance you do not have procedures for every job, go to www.TutorFi. com/procedure-cheat-sheet to download a step by cheat sheet designed to help you create <u>results focused procedures</u> that can transform your company from the inside out.

What you'll discover throughout this book is how to build on those procedures, make employees accountable to them, and track the results.

Assuming you have procedures in place, understand that this alone will not be the factor that propels you to hero status once you implement the plan laid out in this book.

After all, what good are procedures if they are not being followed to the T day in and day out?

To take that a step further, what good are procedures if they are not being measured and improved upon based on specific results focused goals?

The shift that is taught in this book forces you to think about implementing real accountability systems to ensure your procedures are being followed every day.

On top of this, you'll also discover why getting real user feedback is an important foundation for adapting and growing your company to all new heights.

The biggest revelation you will have after reading this book is the fact that you will be able to guarantee a specific result with any training program you create.

The ideas are unlimited:

- Sales training (ex. How to double sales in 90 days)
- New employee training (ex. How to do job from step 1 and on)
- Certification training (ex. Manager, specialist, etc.)
- Customer service training (ex. Phones, online chat, etc.)
- Management training (ex. How to increase team production, sales, co-operation among departments, etc.)
- And any type of result you wish to have…

You'll discover how to use procedures, accountability and feedback to systematically improve every area of your company.

For the first time in company history (probably), you'll be able to guarantee specific results for every department even if your employees work from home.

When it's all said and done, you'll be the reason for your company's sky rocketing success.

Chapter 1

My First
Evolutionary Baby
Step Started Here

G rowing up in Pittsburgh, PA, I never gave much thought about who I wanted to become or what I wanted to do with my life. I skated through public school doing the absolute minimum to maintain my C average and went onto college with no real intention in mind.

My business career started in 1997, when two friends sat me down and showed me a presentation that made perfect sense to me. I chose to enroll myself as a representative for a direct sales company who specialized in discount long-distance calling (back then, most people paid twenty-five cents or more per minute to talk on the phone).

After spending a few months learning the business and being mentored by successful people earning five figures

per month, I started to believe that I could be rich and successful too.

My mentors Bill and Andy would always tell me stories about how other representatives were making millions per month. When I finally got a chance to meet some of these people in person, the belief that I could do it too, sky rocketed.

As I started to gain momentum, this opportunity just seemed so much better than the traditional college path I felt lost in anyways. I didn't even have a major at that point in my life, so I made the decision to take two years off from college so I could focus on building my business.

During this time, we were not using the Internet for marketing and the #1 way to build my business was to invite people to watch a face-to-face business presentation. This was the same method that was used to recruit me and all my friends did, was ask if I was interested in making more money.

After getting some basic training, and overcoming my fear of asking complete strangers if they were interested in making more money, I was able to meet people and invite them to watch a presentation.

Using this method, I was able to recruit dozens of representatives and earn residual income that was paying me pretty well for the small amount of time I was putting in.

I got real good at making friends with strangers and then asking if they knew anyone interested in making more money. Most said, "Yeah, me". From there I would set appointments and present the opportunity.

Out of about five thousand reps in my state, I became one of a handful that made it to the highly regarded Regional Director position. After doing so well at recruiting, the next big success step revolved around me training all my reps to do what I was doing.

The problem I was faced with was the fact that none of my reps felt comfortable doing what I was doing. No matter what type of training or pep talk I gave them, no one had the guts to go up to a complete stranger, strike up a conversation and ask them if they knew anyone who wanted to earn more money.

Instead, they would bug their friends and family, who of course shot them down. Following that demoralizing experience, most reps just stopped asking anyone and eventually quit.

This was disheartening to me, because I recruited them with the promise of helping each representative make more money. I began to feel as if I was failing them and truthfully, that became a theme in life for many more years to come. That uncomfortable feeling is what drove me.

I learned how embrace that feeling and became even more determined to help my reps secure a steady stream of pre-qualified leads without ever bugging strangers or their friends and family again.

As this was all going on in my mind, I realized that if I could train my reps to recruit in a fun way, this would be a huge opportunity for me to earn a monthly residual income too. This was going to be a true win/win.

The communications company I was involved with at the time promised us an opportunity to get in on the deregulation

of utilities which would allow home owners to have more than one choice for electricity, water, gas, phone and more.

The overall plan really helped me to see how the residual model could work once I had thousands of customers using our long distance service. After all, it would be easy to ask those same customers to save more money on other utilities.

This sent me on a quest to help my representatives anyway I could. Since they were not good at setting up meetings, I had to figure out a way to bring interested people right to them. On top of that, I had to train them to be successful with the new method I would teach.

Chapter 2

THE REAL
EVOLUTION
BEGINS...

The first oddball method I started out with was called "littering the streets". I would spend 10 hours a day placing business cards that said Need More Money? Call 800#.

I put these cards on super markets bulletin boards, pay phones (yes there were lots of payphones back then), libraries, cars, doors, mailboxes and more.

People would call the 800# if they were interested. On this phone line there was a recorded message that they would listen to. If they liked what they heard, they would leave their name and number for a follow up call.

Once I put this system into place, I solved the riddle of how to generate leads from people who were really interested.

This was a big moment in my life because this experience helped me gain confidence in myself again.

I spent time perfecting this new method of recruiting. Once I got the prospects information from the recorded call, I would call to follow up and set up a meeting A.S.A.P.

With this new system in place, I was able to enroll more reps than ever before. For a moment, I celebrated, but then realized that in order to become a real leader, I had to train my recruits how to do what I was doing.

This is when I realized that none of my recruits were littering the streets like they promised. At first I was confused by this, because each rep I recruited swore they would litter the streets just like I was doing. After asking the right questions, I discovered that my reps were not comfortable doing this on their own.

This forced me to get more involved with my training approach. I started to meet reps in towns where they lived so we could litter the streets together. Every time, I did this type of training which was nothing more than hand holding, it worked and the reps were able to recruit others into the business.

Those moments excited me, but if I was not with each of my recruits, guiding them in that manner, they would never go out on their own to litter the streets. They would be lucky to put out ten cards per week, on their way out of the grocery store.

No matter what type of coaching or incentives I offered up, my reps would not commit to littering the streets unless I

was there with them. My first training program failed because I could not be there for every rep I recruited.

Chapter 3

THE EVOLUTION CONTINUES...

I was down, but not out. The internet started to come to life in 1998,and I found a company who claimed they could generate leads from prospects that filled out an online form and expressed a real interest in starting a part-time business.

I was really excited for this new opportunity. I knew that once I could give my reps hot leads that already had an interest in making more money, this would be the solution I dreamt about! After all, this was way easier than walking around and placing opportunity cards all over town. Heck, now they didn't even have to leave home.

But before I could recommend this lead generation program to each rep, I had to prove that my new system could work.

I stayed up late one night writing a script that I would use and record onto a cassette tape recorder (another old school technology you might not have ever seen). The next day, I recorded my voice as I read the script. I was very excited and believed that my message would get people to sign up for my business opportunity on the spot.

I was finally ready to test this new system. As I called through the leads, 50% would tell me that they never filled out a form requesting information on a part-time business, 25% would hang up and 20% would hang up in a very rude manner.

The 5% that were somewhat interested agreed to listen to my fifteen minute tape-recorded presentation. Every time someone said yes, I would get chills up and down my spine and then race to place the tape recorder next to the phone. I then walked away as my prospect listened.

After that and *if* they were still on the phone line (about ½ would hang up during the recording), I would ask them a direct yes or no question. "Would you like to start your business today?". If they said yes, I would ask for their credit card info, enroll them and teach them the same system.

The best part is that they were being trained from the very first call, because they would be required to do exactly what I did to recruit other reps.

I finally had a duplicable system and my close rate was right at the 50% mark for anyone who listened to the entire recording.

I finally created a system to help my reps be successful and training them was a piece of cake. All they had to do was call the leads, follow my script and allow the recording to make the sale.

This was also the first time I created a training program that produced a specific quantified result. It took about 40 calls to generate a new rep.

I trained with my reps by role-playing the script with them and I even let them listen on the other line as I called leads.

My training program worked perfectly as long as each rep was committed to calling the leads. As it turned out, many of my 'excited at the time' recruits quickly fizzled out because they couldn't accept the no's, hang-ups, and rude people that came along with the system.

I tried to put a positive spin on the negativity of calling leads, hoping to encourage and inspire my reps to commit themselves to calling leads five nights a week like I was.

I proved this model could be successful for me, but it wasn't successful for my newly recruited reps. When I realized my coaching was not good enough, I was sick to my stomach. No matter how hard I coached and encouraged each rep, they just couldn't get over the number of "no's" it took to get a "yes".

After realizing this, I couldn't even muster the will to call leads myself anymore. It just didn't feel right. Even if I recruited a new rep, my training program for success just wasn't good enough to help them earn money like I had promised. I felt like a complete failure and once again, it hurt me deep down inside.

Chapter 4

MY EVOLUTION
STOPPED COLD
IN ITS TRACKS

O n top of my failure, and after two years of hard work, the direct sales company I was so dedicated to, closed their doors forever. I was forced to take a step back and really look at my life.

This is when I made the decision to go back to college to get my Health and Physical Education degree.

After being down on myself for a few months, I was able to feel better and get myself excited about the possibility of being a health and physical educator (a fancy way of saying I was going to become a gym teacher). At least I could wake up every day and have fun. That was truly a job I would love.

I enrolled back into college, but I did not give up on my dream of running my own business and having the freedom

11

to do what I wanted, when I wanted. That seed was already planted in my mind.

My direct sales experience was indeed a great one even though it ended in misery as my company flopped and I failed miserably at training and coaching the reps I recruited.

Thinking back, my mentors Bill and Andy from my old company did an excellent job of convincing me that I could make millions in my sleep. The thought of working when I wanted and if I wanted was embedded deep in my heart.

During my time in college, I read dozens of business and self-help books, and attended many business seminars and also business college talks. I even took some business and MBA classes that had nothing to do with my Health and Physical Education degree.

I was transforming myself in a big way until one day I realized I had no money. My student loans ran out and it was time to get a real job to support myself through college. This realization was very disheartening, since it was only a year ago when I thought I was going to be a millionaire.

After an extensive interview, I ended up landing an oddball job through a marketing company that let me work on weekends. I was put in charge of promoting Pro Plan dog food at six different Pet Smart stores around the Pittsburgh area. I hired people to set up a booth and we gave out coupons to entice people to try this new, premium dog food.

I remember thinking one day that I couldn't believe they picked me for this job. At the time, I didn't have any training or management experience, but looking back on it, I did have

that winning, I'll get it done attitude and I think that's why they chose me.

Either way, the pressure was on and they were measuring the sales that came directly from the coupons of each store.

Chapter 5

IT FELT GOOD TO
EVOLVE AGAIN...

I began to train my six weekend employees by showing them how it was done. I concentrated on three simple steps:

1. Making a friend
2. Educating the customer on the benefits of the dog food
3. Asking if they would buy pro plan with the coupon (this required a yes or no response)

After demonstrating how to do it with my employees, I would watch them follow the script and get the same result. I also had them track stats on "yes's" and "no's" to make sure they were asking every customer they spoke with.

After I trained my team, I would drive around to all the different stores and check on them during the weekends. My employees knew I held them accountable for sales and when I walked in, the first thing I would do was look at the stat sheet.

There were times in the beginning when I needed to coach my employees up a bit and that's what I did, but in a fun way. I would observe their approach and offer both positive and negative feedback when needed.

Once my employees gained confidence and momentum, they were able to sustain high sales numbers every weekend. The best part is, they loved their jobs and we were all having fun!

Within three months, my six stores were moving so many bags of Pro Plan that Purina and the marketing company I was working for invited me to Purina headquarters just outside of St. Louis. It seemed like they rolled out the red carpet for me as I got a first class tour of the facility, dinner at the finest restaurant and extra training on all the ways they studied and improved their dog food formulas.

The big shock happened when they offered me a job as the head trainer. They wanted me to train other managers who were doing what I was doing in other cities.

I had to tell them no because I was not prepared to quit school when I only had one more year to go. They countered by offering me extra money to travel on weekends and train managers in other cities on Saturdays and Sundays. I said yes.

During those few months, I discovered none of the other city managers were as scripted and systematized as I was. I

implemented the same system I did with my Pittsburgh stores and those managers were able to duplicate my success.

When I left each city with my system in place, those stores sales sky rocketed and I was praised week after week on our conference calls. I was having a lot of fun and making good money while still finishing up college.

It was about six months later when my job was terminated because the marketing company I was working for lost the contract. I never found out the exact reason they lost the contract, but my guess is that they didn't implement my training program soon enough and Purina could not justify paying them anymore.

I knew I gave them 100% of my effort and because of that, I managed to hold my head up high even though my job was terminated. At that time, I didn't know how I was going to earn money, but I was dedicated to finishing out my collegiate career with a degree.

During my last year of college, I became really confident in my abilities as I started getting straight A's. I could feel the success that was heading my way.

I decided to try selling products on the Internet, but I was not sure what to sell. In many of the books I read, it was stated to sell things that people want, not what they need. So I decided to enter the beauty market since everyone wants to look beautiful.

This was the beginning of the Internet age and I was reading and learning from Internet marketing pioneers who taught me how to create a simple website and sell, sell, sell.

After realizing I could have the American dream and make money without actually working, I found some unique spa products and started selling them online.

During the final year of my collegiate career and while I was student teaching, I was able to earn more money selling my products than I would have been earning if I chose to go into teaching. It was crazy how fast the money started to roll in.

I remember walking into the teachers lounge and thinking *Wow, I make more money than every teacher in the teachers lounge.* That realization was truly something I've dreamt about for years and there I was doing it.

I was having the time of my life waking up every day and going to school where I was student teaching. At the same time, I was learning how to train the people whom I hired to help me. It was impossible for me to grow my business on my own while I was student teaching five days a week.

Chapter 6

FORCED
EVOLUTION

Healthy Revelations was on pace to sell over two million dollars worth of products in 2003. I was hiring helpers and training them the best I could. Before I knew it, I had a team of people helping me run my first million-dollar company while I was finishing college.

My team would ship, answer phones, and respond to customer emails almost 24 hours a day. I was constantly getting feedback from my team and implementing new scripts for them to test, while doing my best to teach my new home-based shipping department how to ship products in a professional manner.

On top of this, I was learning so much while teaching gym and health to my students. The best part about the spring of

2003 was not the money that was rolling in, but my student teaching experience and the lessons I was forced to learn.

During the first two weeks of student teaching, I was instructed to observe my mentor teacher, Mark. He had been teaching for twenty-two years and currently taught gym and health classes to 7th, 8th and 9th graders.

Teaching gym to middle school kids was probably the best training and coaching education I could have ever received. While being the leader of fifty to a hundred students at one time might not sound all that challenging to you, I can assure you that most of those students didn't think of gym class as fun and those same students would challenge me every day in front of their peers.

As I slowly took over the gym class, my teacher eventually ducked out into his office and sometimes did not come back for the rest of the day.

I was on my own and I loved the challenge. My lesson plans were spot on every day. Before each class, I would remind my students that we were here to have fun, learn or improve a sports skill.

I would never allow students to get picked last, and for any student who felt embarrassed about their lack of a sporting skill, I would give them one on one attention while getting them to relax, laugh, and have fun as they learned something new.

My lessons were always focused on an end result—throwing a football, catching a baseball, running a ¼ mile etc. During these drills, I was challenged by some students who would tell me "I can't". I would always counter that statement by making them say, "How can I?".

I would enforce that rule for all of my students and when those doubtful words came out of any student's mouth, they would be forced to repeat that statement with "How can I?".

For the students who did not want to follow along and tried to become disruptive, those situations only happened one time. After I dealt with the disruption at the moment it happened, the other students went with the flow.

Some of the kids actually called me Sargent and sort of thought of me in that manner. I felt like most of the kids liked and respected me, but some sort of hated me because I would always ask them for more effort and would not accept laziness.

Sometimes, I would spend time teaching a skill to a student who had no interest in learning it. I felt compelled to coach my students to at least have most of the skills required to play in the games we played after each of the drills were taught.

When game time did finally come, I always made the games fun by dividing up the teams equally. For the last point, run or touchdown, I always implemented Metric Rules. Metric Rules was something that my high school gym teacher implemented and simply stated the last run, touchdown or point wins. If one team was up 10–1 and the team with only 1 point scored the next point, they were declared the winners.

I enjoyed teaching gym and most of my students enjoyed it too. When it came to health class, this was a completely different story.

Every student got an A in gym class as long as they put forth effort, but I when I took over Health class, I was shocked to see that 1 in 4 students were failing and another 1/4th had a D average.

This concerned me in a big way. When I asked Mark about it, he blamed the student's poor grades on laziness. I decided I was going to be an inspiration to the failing students and help them turn things around.

I devised a plan and began teaching class in a more exciting way. Each lesson was interactive. We had class discussions and I constantly called on students who were not paying attention.

The next few weeks were a struggle! I tried reaching out to several of the failing students and even spent time with a few before and after class. I was trying to boost their moral any way I could.

Many of the students thought of themselves as failures and would not even attempt to learn the information. Even when called on in class, most disinterested students would just say, "I don't know".

Each day was more frustrating than the day before. My patience was running thin.

After three weeks of teaching, I felt like a complete failure. Nothing seemed to help these students learn!

My frustration led me to ask all 200 of my afternoon students how I could become a better teacher. Most students told me they just got bored in the classroom, because they didn't want to learn about health. They said it just wasn't fun.

Some joked with me about creating video game lessons and some even pulled out their hand held video games during these discussions just to show me. Every student jumped at the idea of learning in the computer room when I presented it.

I decided to reserve the computer room for the next health lesson. Looking back on it now, this one decision to

try something new changed my perspective on traditional teaching, coaching and all training methods as well as my future as an educator.

That night, I bought a new domain name and I put together an entertaining health web site that presented information in a one by one format so the students could read each webpage and click to read the next one.

Some pages just had cool images of the heart, lungs and other health related systems. Other pages had written information that the students were required to read. I even made it more entertaining by adding color, bold, and different engaging elements into each page.

I also reduced all paragraphs to no more than five sentences max so it was easy to read and the students could feel like they accomplished something as they scrolled through each page.

Another secret I picked up on was that by adding some curiosity about the next section, the students showed a bit more excitement to move forward. For the most part, I was writing and summarizing the health information out of the book. The only difference was that I made each section more exciting than the actual textbook.

This took a lot of my time and honestly, I don't know why I was so committed, but this strategy was a huge success. I got more compliments during these first few lessons than I had ever gotten in my life. And the kids loved me for it!

This noticeable spark of interest encouraged me in a big way!

As my student teaching experience progressed, I spent extra time at home preparing online tutorials. Sometimes I would stay up all night and only get one or two hours of sleep.

My hard work paid off as I taught my last few Health classes using even more unique online tools including animated images (this was a really cool function back then). The students absolutely loved it! Even more importantly, they became more engaged learners.

Even those students who were "too cool" or "too shy" were participating in class. Most students actually enjoyed learning in the computer room and would discuss openly the subjects I brought up during what was now computer room discussions (no more classroom discussions).

When my student teaching experience was over, I helped most of my 7th, 8th and 9th graders pass health without any grade curving. The computer room discovery was truly a breakthrough and I could not get this breakthrough out of my mind.

After finally getting my college degree and experiencing what it was like to teach, I discovered my real passion.

I was earning five figures per month with my Healthy Revelations company, and I wanted to invest my profits into something I was more excited about. After all, the only reason I chose beauty products is because that's what people were spending their money on.

After experiencing such a huge breakthrough in the computer room with my students, I had an itch to go after something bigger.

My mind was racing with ideas and I remember boldly proclaiming to some friends that I would create an entire industry. This was the way my mind was programmed to operate and I put my money where my mouth was.

I decided to take my profits from my Healthy Revelations company and reinvest them into an online tutoring website designed to help students learn from their computer. At the time, this made perfect sense.

Even back then, students were overly stimulated by television, the Internet and video games.

Imagine how focused you would have been on your schoolwork if you had these distractions to deal with everyday. Now fast forward into the Facebook and smart phone era. This makes it even harder to focus.

You probably agree with me and understand that things needed to change in order to adapt to the ways students prefer to learn. My goal was to help as many students as possible achieve better grades, attitude and self-confidence.

Chapter 7

WHEN
EVOLUTION
FEELS RIGHT,
GO FOR IT...

I took my passion for teaching students and created a uniquely effective, personal online tutoring solution.

In the summer of 2003, I spent long hours consulting with programmers, researching different technologies and working to create an online learning system designed to get students excited about learning.

After about six months with minimal sleep, it was complete!

I'm talking about a real, honest-to-goodness, interactive, *virtual classroom*. A place with all the tools a tutor needs to do their job without the distractions found in a brick and mortar school.

From my passion, and with the help of a programming partner, Ehomeworkhelp.com was created (see front page

newspaper article below). Our technology was so new that our small town of Indiana, PA picked up on us quickly. We even landed on the front page of the Indiana Gazette with over 50,000 readers.

The idea was truly a breakthrough in the tutoring industry and many parents were interested in enrolling their children. The training and coaching of our newly hired tutors ended up being our biggest challenge.

First, we interviewed our tutors and chose the winners based on experience, willingness to adapt to new online learning technology and their passion for being a great tutor.

Then we began training and coaching each tutor inside the online classroom until they got familiar with the online tutoring tools that were built into the whiteboard application.

Following this, we role-played with each tutor as if we were the student. Once the tutor felt comfortable, we scheduled each tutor to work between the hours of 3pm midnight eastern time.

Since this was a homework help service, our members could log on at anytime during business hours and our tutors were standing by ready to help students with their homework.

I'll never forget the ding, ding, ding sound that our computers made when members logged on. My partner and I would jump up and make sure a tutor picked up the student and took them into the online classroom. Once inside, we would cross our fingers and hope it all worked out well.

For the most part it did. Every now and then a student would have a problem that was too complex for the tutor and in a situation like this, we would have to schedule a time for them to meet with a different tutor.

Before we knew it, we were busy signing up new student accounts while other interested parents were calling us daily to inquire about our service. We had a pipeline of clients coming to us from a variety of different online advertisements.

After about three months, we realized we were not making any money. The members who signed up were not sticking around, and it continued to cost us a fortune to advertise on the Internet.

I began calling parents directly after they canceled our service to ask them why they canceled, or if there was something we could have done better.

Most gave a lame excuse telling me their child didn't need homework help anymore, but many parents told me they would like it if their child could work with the same tutor again and again instead of getting a different tutor every time.

Chapter 8

WHEN CLIENTS REQUEST A MORE PERSONAL APPROACH (AND THEY WILL), EVOLVE TO SERVE THEM

I n late 2003, I bought out my former partner and moved away from a homework help service altogether.

In 2004, I fumbled with an online tutoring company called Live eTutor and learned another valuable lesson.

After doing more exit interviews as I was losing more money, I discovered that parents not only wanted a personal tutor for their child, but they also wanted an academic consultant they could count on to help guide their child's education.

In 2005, I changed the name again and rolled out a national advertising campaign proclaiming, *OwlOnlineTutoring.com takes the time to care unlike any tutoring organization out there*. If you go to the website, you'll see my original video that helped launch this incredibly popular service.

With my small but dedicated team, we began tutoring a handful of students in a brand new way. Our new tutors were more engaging and helped each student have fun while learning.

I hired and trained a Director of Academic Affairs, who focused her time on following up with parents, while making sure their sons and daughters were improving their grades, attitude and confidence.

With my new "Owl Online Tutoring Company" this marked the first time we focused on over delivering to the parents and taking the time to care. It was paying off.

My company was finally profitable and parents were lining up to pay for our service. The students loved their personalized etutoring sessions, but it was getting hard to keep up. We were just growing too fast for my small team to handle. The stress was overwhelming.

Some of my tutors were tutoring one student after another all night long, while feeling pressure to be the best tutor they could be. As they got stressed out, the caring and quality of each session went downhill.

I was trying my best to hire and train more tutors, but it took a long time to train them well enough for me to trust them to deliver perfect online tutoring sessions.

My Director of Academic Affairs was getting stressed out too and the parents could feel the stress during their consultations. "This just isn't what I signed up for", my director told me. I felt horrible and didn't know what to do.

Here I was doing what I planned on doing and people from all walks of life were lined up and offering to give me money. In

some cases a lot of money so they could learn what they could not learn in a classroom!

I soon realized there was no way OwlOnlineTutoring.com could ever meet such a great demand.

The whole industry... the one we all but created... had grown too monumental proportions and everything I promised was not happening. This situation made my stomach churn once again.

Chapter 9

STRESS WILL FORCE
EVOLUTION UPON YOU

After stopping all advertising for OwlOnlineTutoring. com, I decided to change my entire business model.

First, I had to remove the position of Director of Academic Affairs. Even though parents did appreciate my director's expertise, they would appreciate it more if their child's tutor consulted with them directly instead of having us in the middle of it.

In order to ensure each tutor really cared and over delivered to both parents and students, I made the decision to allow tutors to operate their own businesses. We gave them their own online classroom and scheduling tools that made tutoring online easy.

My gut told me that tutors would care more about their clients needs if their income depended on it. Once I gave our

new tutors the tools to run their own businesses, it took all of the pressure off me and my team.

Plus, this was more of a win/win/win for tutors, parents and tutor. Parents finally got the personal academic consultant they wanted. Students were able to feel extra comfortable getting tutoring from the same tutor, who focused on teaching and having fun. Tutors were forced to care and were finally able to earn the type of money they deserved ($25 - $75 per hour).

The whole idea felt absolutely perfect and, I launched TutorFi.com in 2007. Before I knew it, I had a steady stream of tutors paying $97 per month to be apart of our trusted online tutoring community.

As new tutors enrolled, we would set up their accounts that had our online tutoring tools pre-installed for them. From there, we assumed these tutors who paid us to start their businesses would do what they were already doing in the face to face tutoring world. The only difference now was the fact that they could tutor students online from home.

It was a big shocker when I realized most of our tutors did not tutor a single student, and the majority quit three months after they signed up. They could not justify the price since they were not making any money tutoring students online. The worst part was that many of the tutors that quit were blaming us for their failure.

After exit interviewing those tutors who cancelled their membership, I discovered that none of them had business experience and they had no clue how to find parents who would invest in their child's education.

This inspired me to write my first book called the "*Blueprint For Online Tutoring Success*". Inside this book, I trained tutors how they could start and succeed with their online tutoring business by simply taking action on each of the lessons within the chapters.

I covered everything from having a professional web presence to marketing and even included my phone scripts that were proven to be successful with my previous online tutoring companies. I even gave examples of my own successes and failures in advertising so each client could learn from my mistakes.

I felt so good after my book was completed and I knew that once my tutors read through the book, success would be just around the corner. There was no doubt about it!

Right about at the same time, I got my hands on the most powerful book I have ever read. It's called the *4 - Hour Workweek* by Timothy Ferris.

As I turned the pages, I resonated with every word that was written. This book was almost an exact story of what I was going through and as I read more, I realized this was a story of where I wanted to go.

Even though I was not exactly sure how I could apply everything I learned; my brain was on fire with ideas and ways I could outsource every detail of both of my businesses while living out my dreams. At that time, if one of my key employees went down, I was screwed. I knew that for sure!

Over the next year, I started to think in a whole new way. The ideas came pouring out of my head. Tim's book really

opened my mind to new ways of thinking. I felt like something big was about to happen, but I didn't know what.

Chapter 10

WRITING A BOOK WAS NOT GOOD ENOUGH—EVOLUTION FORCED ME TO ENSURE MY CLIENTS ACHIEVED SUCCESS NO MATTER WHAT

Now that my book was being given to insiders who purchased my TutorFi membership, I knew the success stories would be piling up. After all, I was giving them the tools and a step-by-step blueprint for success.

As new TutorFi members joined, I expected most to stay with our program forever since they would have my book in their hands and would easily be able to justify $97 per month from even just one monthly student account which averaged $250.

Over the next six months, I watched and observed carefully. Sadly, the exact same thing was happening then as it did before. Most tutors were not sticking with my program because they were not earning enough money to justify the costs.

I was perplexed.

The entire point of writing my book was to help tutors be successful. On top of this, I was offering every tool possible to help tutors become successful. The fact that 90% of them were still canceling within three months was disturbing to me. I really thought hard on what to do next and then it came to me.

I ended up teaming with one of our super start clients Gretchen Touchard. She started off as a TutorFi member and loved TutorFi so much that she wanted to help out in a big way. With her background as a health and educational coach, she headed up TutorFi's new coaching department. This is when we officially added coaching as part of our program.

Gretchen started off by calling our members to make sure they were reading the book and most importantly, taking action!

It became evident rather quickly that we had made the right decision. The business instantly improved and tutors started staying on well over the three-month mark. We also started receiving heart-felt emails thanking us for TutorFi and our wonderful coach Gretchen.

I was amazed that the personal element made that much of a difference. It seemed most clients just didn't have the confidence to take action on their own, but the moment someone was coaching and caring about their success, their entire attitude changed.

Over the next year and into 2009, TutorFi gained momentum. Most tutors where staying on month after month and new tutors were joining us one after the other.

Our new business model was working out well, but there was still a lot of room for improvement. Even though most of

our tutors were staying with us for six months and longer, some of the tutors who were canceling their memberships after paying monthly for so long, were getting angry with us. This seemed to be a reoccurring theme ever since the launch of TutorFi.

These tutors were still blaming us for their lack of success!

As we examined each case individually, we did find one correlation. These tutors who were complaining, were not speaking with their coach and rarely even replied to Gretchen's outgoing phone calls or emails.

As these angry rants came to us one by one, Gretchen would simply ask why they never allowed her to coach them and she also reminded each tutor that it was their choice to not read the book and not take action on the lessons within.

Usually that type of reply would calm the tutor down and let them take responsibility for their own failure, which was really nothing more than them deciding to quit and not take action.

Other times, we would have to refund members just to avoid further conflict. This didn't sit well with us.

Even though I was taken back by some of these incidents, as a business owner I learned to always take responsibility no matter what. It was not the client's fault for not making money; it was mine for not training them properly.

This type of thinking forced me to brainstorm different ways we could create a step-by-step training & coaching program to make sure each tutor was successful if they did the work.

The type of coaching program I was thinking of, would be way different from just handing our clients a book and talking

with them over the phone every couple weeks. The program I was dreaming of had to have real accountability steps in place to ensure success for our clients.

Chapter 11

I EVOLVED SO MUCH THAT IT ONLY FELT RIGHT TO OFFER A *Power Guarantee* - A MONEY BACK GUARANTEE ON MAKING MONEY

To start off this chapter, I feel it's important to speak more about being responsible. This was a big area of my life that I improved on in my thirties, and the result of this new way of thinking lead me down a road that I am so grateful to have traveled and continued to travel on.

The fact that I did not blame my tutors for their own failures forced me to use my brain and collaborate with friends, colleagues, partners and others who had a tremendous impact on steering me to where I am now.

This new way of thinking has been spoken about in dozens of books I read and mentors I learned from. It seems that once a person is able to take responsibility for every problem that creeps up in life, they are taken to a higher

level of living that forces their mind to create solutions out of thin air.

Taking responsibility is what forced me to change the entire TutorFi business model and have the guts to guarantee results for my tutors.

The reality is, I don't want anyone's money unless I can provide them real value. If a tutor was not able to make money with my program after doing the work that was required, I didn't feel right accepting their money.

Plus, once I had the nerve to guarantee results, I could charge way more money for that type of guarantee and the promise of success.

Every part of that idea made perfect sense, but I was not sure how to implement such a program. There was no way to guarantee success from reading my book alone, because I couldn't expect my coach to watch and review every detail as the tutor hopefully followed my blueprint for online tutoring business success.

I spent a lot of time reviewing different online tools and software, but did not find any solutions that fit the new accountability and results based success model I was dreaming of. Most of the software out there was automated and not personal enough.

I wanted to have tasks at the end of each module or lesson that forced each client to do the work and then show it to their coach. From there, I envisioned the coach being able to give feedback and send the next lesson.

The best way I found of implementing this type of program back in 2009 was to use an auto responder email system where

we could automatically send the lesson and have instructions for each client to respond to their coach via an email reply.

I went to work immediately. I took each chapter in my book and created a lesson out of each one. In some of the lessons, I created videos to better explain things that were written in the book.

I sent 2 emails at a time. The first had the detailed lesson and second was to be replied to and emailed directly to their coach while showing their work inside that email.

As the ideas kept flowing, I knew I would have to come back into the auto responder messages and change some of the lessons based on user feedback, which brings me to another point. The accountability solution I was dreaming of made me as equally as accountable as the client.

So as long as I could edit my email lessons based on feedback, I would always be able to improve the program to ensure success.

Once I set this up, our new training program was live and tutors were enrolled into our brand new "Fill Your Practice Training Program". I used the auto responder to send one lesson every seven days through email.

As tutors started going through our training, the feedback was great!

Tutors loved the lessons and were following along pretty well. Gretchen was receiving email replies with the work that had been completed, and she would schedule coaching calls a couple times per month with each member.

After a month of testing and using our new system, we found two major flaws.

The first flaw revolved around Gretchen responding to the answers that each tutor provided in the reply email. She was communicating with tutor's via email, but it got difficult for her to keep track of who was doing what and if they got it right the first time.

She tried keeping track of each tutor's progress using spreadsheets, but this was not an efficient way to operate and it was hard to keep up with each tutor's progress while she was busy coaching and responding to other tutors.

The second major flaw was the fact that some of our tutors would receive an email for lesson five when they were not even done with lesson two. In a perfect world, they would not even see lesson five unless the coach approved them to receive it because they proved competence and took action on the required task in that particular lesson.

It was at this time when I realized I would need to build a permanent solution to our training & coaching program. The auto responder system I set up was not working out the way I had hoped.

Even though my idea failed, I knew I was on the right track with my thinking. I was being forced to evolve again and it felt darn good. I was really starting to embrace the evolution process.

I knew that if I could create a results focused accountability system, I could use it to explode TutorFi and outsource all the jobs for both of my companies. By having systems like this set up, I could live the true 4-hour workweek lifestyle.

Chapter 12

EVOLUTION
FULL CIRCLE

As TutorFi was growing, I began planning and overseeing the creation of my new dream lifestyle software. This new tool would allow me to live the lifestyle I wanted and help more people get results. It was a true win/win.

I decided to name my creation Evolutionary Training & Coaching Software (ETC Software), because I had to evolve so much as a person to finally take 100% responsibility for my client's success.

The idea was to take my book and break it down into lessons while spoon-feeding each idea to members one lesson at a time. At the end of the lesson, they would have to prove their knowledge and show the action they took before their coach graduated them *manually* onto the next lesson.

I wanted to have questions and tasks at the end of each lesson/module that forced each client to do the work, or answer the questions and then show it to their coach.

From there, I envisioned the coach being able to manually graduate each client from one lesson to the next. Progression would only take place if the client showed competence when answering the questions and completing the tasks that were required.

This solution I was dreaming of had to involve a real person who would be responsible for deciding *if* the client would move forward in the training or not. If the coach allowed someone to move forward without answering questions or doing the work properly, they would be responsible for that mistake and not the client.

Essentially, my clients, my coaches and me (the expert/ creator of the program) all had to be responsible for this solution to really be able to deliver the end result which in my case came down to helping tutors make money as an online tutor.

I was getting more and more excited as I planned out each important part of this evolutionary software I was going to create.

I knew that once I put my "Fill Your Practice" training program in place using my new software, TutorFi would be able to grow without me even being present. Plus, I would be able to peek in at anytime to see the progress and communication of any client or coach.

Before any new coaches even got started working for TutorFi, they would be required to complete a certification program Gretchen and I would create using my software. Once

this was set up, there would be no doubt that I would be able to fully trust all of my coaches to present and teach my program the way it was intended.

The goal with both of these programs was to produce certified coaches who would help tutors become successful by simply following the step-by-step program I created. As I was planning all of this, I wanted to investigate how other experts currently taught their information, and if they had coaches who taught their material too.

It was during this time that I became even more interested in learning from experts in other fields like business, personal development, motivation, and other important subjects I needed to know more about. I began an in depth study on how each expert presented their information and of course the information itself.

I invested over $20,000 in 2009 on personal coaching, membership sites, conferences, webinars, DVD's, and more.

The education I received was worth way more than the money I paid, but as I experienced all these different forms of training and mingled in the different online communities, I realized that I was in the small minority of people who took action on what was being taught.

This was even more true with people I met at conferences and seminars. They would come to the event with their hopes and dreams on the top of their minds. They would then leave each event with an exact plan and way to make it happen.

When I would follow up with my new friends months later (I made a lot of friends and always followed up to support

them), most of them had gotten distracted, started something new, or quit altogether.

I always wondered if the experts selling their seminars, webinars, membership forums, books, DVD's, etc. were bothered by the fact that most of their customers did not take action or truly benefit from their training.

For me personally, it bothered the heck out of me! I even had an in depth conversation with one of my personal business coaches who had a successful coaching practice himself.

In a nutshell, I was told that I should not spend time worrying about the success of others if they did not take action on what was taught.

I knew he was right when he told me that, but what if I could ensure they understood the success steps and took action?

Could I actually promise my tutors a result?

Would that promise place me on top of the industry?

Could I increase my prices in exchange for a promised result?

I pondered these questions for months as I put the framework of the ECT software into place.

Chapter 13

YET ANOTHER EVOLUTIONARY TWIST

As I was building my ECT software, I began with only my tutors in mind, but as I sifted through all the information in books, DVD's, membership sites and more, I realized that I had to build this software so that other experts could promise their clients a result too.

I wanted experts (like the ones I've been learning from) to be able to teach their material using the same system I was creating. It made perfect sense since I knew of not a single expert out there who offered this type of accountability and results focused training program.

Sure they had coaching programs that would help some clients succeed, but they did not have true accountability set up, and even if they did, they didn't have the details written out

in a step-by-step format based on real user feedback (so they could edit and improve) to ensure success.

I know I am getting deep on you with that last paragraph, but how many experts do you know that have a program for "X" and can guarantee success?

I know of many authors and coaches who teach Internet marketing and at best they have a set of DVD's or a phone-coaching program in place.

Can any Internet marketing coach out there guarantee real success?

Would they have the guts to guarantee results?

The answer is no and the reason is simple. There are too many moving parts that revolve around the subject of Internet marketing.

Now, if those coaches broke down those subjects into programs, then they could sell a results focused service and charge a fortune for the results they promise.

This would also become a new highly priced source of income they did not have before!

In sticking with this example, an Internet marketing expert could create programs on paid advertising, website conversion, email follow up, how to train employees and more.

Yes, the coach could teach all of those subjects individually, but how could the coach ensure every detail was understood and applied properly unless they practically did or reviewed all the work themselves?

This would not be an efficient way to ensure success and would probably drive the coach nuts. Plus, what if the client

wanted to blame the coach in the case that they were not able to be successful, however that was defined?

This would be an uphill battle for the coach, and most who teach such a broad market like internet marketing know they could not make this type of a bold guarantee, for fear of having to refund all the money spent while losing that time trying to help.

Let's use another example.

Can any self help expert guarantee happiness if a client takes their "How To Be Happy Program"?

I pondered this question for weeks and couldn't think of a single reason any expert out there could *not* guarantee real results for any how-to information, other than the fear of failure.

We are so lucky and blessed to be on planet earth at this time. With this sort of technology, experts can guarantee a result, but the technology can't do it alone.

What this world is screaming for is a mash up of both automation and personalization, and that's exactly what I felt inspired to create.

I first heard the word *mash* up from one of the greatest minds of our time, Marshall Thurber. I attended many of Marshall's seminars and observed how connected to the future he really was (especially in his Future of Business course).

Marshall spent 17 years being mentored by Minster Fuller and W. Edwards Demming who are two of America's business and thinking icons and when he says the world is in need of a mash up, that mixes both automation and personalization, I listened!

We are human beings and 100% automation won't cut it anymore. No one wants to talk to a machine or be given automated feedback time after time.

The world desires personal interaction and when you combine that with accountability, and step-by-step processes designed to help someone achieve their goal, you just created a new asset that can help thousands of people around the world get what they want.

I'll elaborate on this example below.

Let's say I was coaching you through my How To Be Happy Program that I created. In lesson seven I ask you to watch my video on being happy and feeling good even if something you didn't want comes into your life. Then, I ask you to answer the questions and do the work, which will be read, and approved by me, your coach.

In one of these open-ended questions, I ask you to tell me a story about a time when something you did not want, came into your life.

Following this question, I ask for a real life example that proves you were still happy and excited because you knew something good would come out of this initially perceived negative situation.

Understand that in order for you to even have gotten to lesson seven, you would have proved to me that you were becoming happier to get this far into my program.

In this situation and as your coach, I would want to hear a story in which you got bad news and started off in fear because that's what you were accustomed to doing before you started my program.

Then, I would want to hear how quickly you changed your emotion and how did not let that negative thought back into your mind.

I would expect you to tell me how you actually got happy and knew something good was coming out of this initially perceived negative situation.

If you did not have a story like that and you left it blank, you would have to wait to respond until that type of event actually happened. Until then, you would not move on in the program.

Of course you could review the previous lessons, but that's it. You would be focused on creating a true ah-ha moment from an originally perceived negative event.

As a coach of this type of program, who was *guaranteeing happiness*, I would have to know that you truly evolving as a person and could prove it by sharing your real life story. That's why automation alone will *not* work.

I might even put that same question into future lessons so I can see you growing as a person.

This one lesson (no matter how many times I embed it into the program) would force you to be conscious of feeling good no matter what. You would be forced to learn how to take responsibility for every thought, no matter the circumstance.

If you tried to give me an answer that sounded fake or far-fetched, I would engage you in an online conversation so you could explain that situation better.

If you were paying for phone coaching too, I would hop on the phone with you and talk it out.

Only if I felt you had experienced that type of happy feeling and took that type of mental action would I ever graduate you onto the next lesson.

That's accountability and as you can see, there has to be a real human element to make this work.

These ideas came to me as I studied so many great and well-respected experts while building out my ETC software. As I was learning their material, I was taking action and holding myself as accountable as I could. But like I said, I am in the minority of people who would go to those lengths.

I listened to one particular mp3 program so many times that I can honestly say that I listened to all thirteen hours at least fifty times. That's how long it took me to master the information and to be able to apply it to my life.

As for the software, I had to make sure experts could create results focused accountability programs and make adjustments when they saw a flaw.

Learning from mistakes is a good thing, because it allows for the creation of the perfect results focused program that can become a high-ticket service or program for any expert.

The same goes for a trainer promising to increase their team's sales output by 50% in 90 days. Just by going for the big goal will help you develop the result.

But remember that you won't get it right the first time and that's OK. Call it beta testing!

Even with the "Fill Your Practice Training" program I was building, I didn't think I would get every lesson right the first time.

I knew there would be sticky points in the training that I would have to adjust in order to give all users the promise of making money as an online tutor.

Not only was it a challenge to influence experts and trainers to think about results in this new way, but it was also a challenge to create this type of solution. Needless to say, my team of programmers were working hard to create this new mash up software solution.

Could I really put this together how I dreamed it?

Chapter 14

EVOLUTIONARY TRAINING & COACHING SOFTWARE WAS RELEASED

In late 2009 the first version of my ETC software was released. I spent a few hours uploading my existing "Fill Your Practice Training" program (the one I had loaded up into my previous auto responder email system) into the software.

Next, I asked important questions and requested specific tasks to be completed and displayed within the answer section of the software.

I then created a coaching account for Gretchen, and she began coaching our TutorFi members in a whole new way.

We finally had the perfect success system, and we could help more tutors succeed with online tutoring businesses than ever before.

I made important changes to the website that offered our TutorFi membership and the big announcement that we made revolved around the fact that we now guaranteed money making success for our members.

Before we knew it, more tutors were signing up then we could handle. I was forced to put up a waiting list to maintain our high level of service.

At that time, Gretchen was the only coach and our practice buddies were staying busy practicing with tutors inside their own online tutoring classroom.

During this time, we made adjustments to each lesson as we got feedback, and before we knew it, more tutors than we ever dreamed were making money doing what they loved, in the comfort of their own home.

We also created a TutorFi coaching certification program that Gretchen managed. By adding more coaches to our operation, we were able to accept more clients.

The coolest part about our new business model was the fact that we had and still have thousands of tutors on our waiting list. Anytime we want new clients, we simply send out an invitation email for a set number of new tutors and within hours, we are able to fill those spots.

This has allowed TutorFi to grow at a rate we can handle while allowing us to keep the highest level of quality for our training program.

We were having more fun than ever in 2010, and we continued getting valuable feedback from our clients. By getting in depth feedback on ways that would make our program better, we were able to make adjustments to our training program

within the ETC software. Our program was destined to be more than just a coaching program. It was going to be an online community.

I worked with my programmers to create top tabs to the "Fill Your Practice Training" program. This allowed us to build a full-blown membership site while being able to add and adjust any webpage quick, fast, and easy. We simply added top tabs, created the webpage and put content on each webpage. Our new community of members could just click the button they wanted once they logged in.

This was very helpful to our members as we added additional content that we now made easily accessible from within the Fill Your Practice Training program.

Now my clients could access a community forum (we use ning.com and just direct members there), additional resources, parent leads, and more. It was fun deciding what other ways we could add value to our community above and beyond our original training program.

Our clients now had access to every success tool they could ever dream of, all in once place. If they wanted personal training, they would complete lessons from the "Fill Your Practice Training" Program, and their coach would be with them every step of the way.

If they wanted to communicate with other members, they could access our forum. It was all right there and boy did our clients love the additional features!

As I started to see a much bigger picture, I realized these new additions to my software could help any expert in any field, teach their followers in a whole new way.

This also made me think about my ETC software from a corporate training point of view. If experts could use it to help more people get results, I would imagine that companies could use to train their employees in a much more efficient and effective manner.

Chapter 15

EVOLUTION MADE ME RE-THINK CORPORATE TRAINING. IF COMPANIES CAN'T ENSURE SPECIFIC RESULTS, ACTIONS OR ACCOUNTABILITY, WHAT GOOD IS TRAINING AT ALL?

As my ECT software was being perfected, I was spending way too much time hiring, training and coaching new employees for my Healthy Revelations company (a home based business), that was doing over two million in sales year after year.

I started to create training videos that were handed out to new employees, but I had no way to ensure they were following my instructions unless I micro managed them.

The videos I created all revolved around specific details in my business that made a difference to overall profitability. For example, I created videos on how to answer the phones, how to respond to emails from potential customers, how

to resolve customer complaints, how to package & ship products, and more.

The videos ended up being pretty longwinded and in depth because there were so many moving pieces for each job.

For example, when a phone rep answers the phone, the first thing they had to do was identify the type of caller. Once that caller was identified, they needed to read the correct script word for word.

Each trained employee should also have been able to follow the "if this, then that" parts of the script and those were not so easy to follow unless they watched my video multiple times and rewound to re-watch those parts that required "if this, then that" script reading.

When responding to emails, I created templates that could be used for each different type of question. The employee was responsible for answering the question with the correct template while being as human as possible with a well thought out response on top of each templated section.

For my shipping department in charge of mailing out products, they had to identify which of three different thank you letters was to be inserted into each outgoing package. My video also showed how to pay for postage and what situations called for overnight, two day or ground shipping.

I even showed them how the mailing software was used to print postage stickers and I demonstrated how to present the products inside of each package with the thank you letter being the top item. These details mattered! After all, it was my goal to impress the customer at the moment they opened our package.

For customer service reps handling complaints, my #1 priority was to maintain our A rating with the BBB. This meant that each employee had to identify the type of complaint whether it was a shipping question, non-receipt of merchandise, product question or a product complaint.

From there, I had to give them enough information in my training videos so they could follow my exact instructions and ensure each customer was happy with the outcome.

Of course I provided documents along with each video, but overseeing this type of training and trusting that every detail was getting accomplished the way it needed to be, was impossible.

I felt trapped. The few key employees I could trust were a product of years of training and follow up by me personally. If any of them went down, I had no way to replace or back them up other than with me.

To make matters worse, now that I was running two companies, I did not have time to train new employees to help grow Healthy Revelations the same intimate way I had trained my key employees who headed up each specific department.

I did attempt to give my key employees the role of manager/ trainer and even let some of them hire their own helpers; but that was a complete disaster.

They spent too much time talking on the phone, sending emails and using other non-productive ways to train someone who is not at your side (Remember, all of my employees were working from home).

Even after shelling out thousands of extra dollars for hours rendered by my managers, I still did not have perfectly trained

employees. Costly mistakes continued to happen and it seemed like the training just never ended.

It would have taken at least six months for their new helpers to know the details well enough to be able to back up or possibly run the entire department on their own, if required.

The main reason I pulled the plug on this idea was because the cost and the inefficiency were just too much. Plus, it gave me a queasy feeling in my stomach every time I heard about the mistakes and extra training required to fix them.

Although my managers did their best trying to train our new employees, they did not do a good job of presenting the details that each helper needed to know in order to do their job to the way it needed to be done.

I also recognized the fact that my trainers did not have good methods for delivering the training, or making each employee accountable for doing their job right. After all, they did not have time to police every phone call, email, or other task, because they were still required to help with day-to-day operations too. The managing was just something I added on.

I still felt stuck. If one of my key employees from any major department went down for any reason, I would lose thousands of dollars a month until a new head of department was trained properly and able to take over.

For example, if my shipping department manager went down, I would have to scramble to fill their shoes and would probably end up doing shipping myself until I found another shipping solution.

Even if I hired someone, my wonderful videos showing how to package my unique products would never be enough to

help them grasp each detail unless I was standing next to them with this current model.

The bottom line was, I just did *not* have a way to police accountability.

I would have had to either throw them into the fire, and hoped they grasped my video lessons, or held their hands and micro-manage every detail while I stayed by their side. It was A or B.

It was during this crisis realization that I discovered the solution was right in front of my eyes.

The same ETC software I was developing for my "Fill Your Practice Training" program for tutors could also be used to train my employees within my, Healthy Revelations company. This would give me so much peace of mind.

My software did not only have to be a coaching platform, but it could also be used and relied upon to train my employees for specific jobs. The best part is that it would allow my managers to manage efficiently and I could just peek into the software to make sure everything was going well.

The ETC platform also allowed easy upload of all secure documents to one place. That helped create a sense of community where all employees could access training or sensitive information securely.

I was excited to try it with my own company to see if I could make this work. The real test was to find out if I could create a program and allow my heads of department to become managers and train my new employees on the details I knew were important to the bottom line.

At this point, my mind was pretty well trained on how to create programs in a step-by-step format so my users could focus on a specific result while having accountability steps in place. I just needed to take that same philosophy and make it applicable for employees to be trained on specific job related tasks.

This art did take some time to get good at, because I had to get real user feedback in order to learn what worked best for different types of training. This process helped me develop my new way of thinking and was the reason why I got so good at creating great programs sooner than later.

Once I understood how most users think and acted when training information was presented, I also discovered what hot buttons to use to elicit a certain response.

Most of my training modules used priming and framing techniques to teach my employees the right way from the very beginning.

If I did not use these techniques, it would have been easy for my employee to get angry or annoyed with a customer.

Priming was used to focus my employees on having fun while interacting with our customer's and this helped facilitate mostly enjoyable conversations or emails.

Framing was used to focus my employees on making sure the customer was always happy with the outcome. Our goal here was to maintain their loyalty and likeliness of them telling someone else about or company.

I applied these techniques to every job-training module including shipping.

Some of my questions would require a simple yes or no answer while others would require an emotional written

response. Other questions would require the work to be shown in the answer section, to ensure true mastery.

After doing the work and completing a training program for every job that my key employees did in their specific departments, I put my first company training programs into action.

I spent time creating the ads to hire the best employees and this one secret I am about to tell you, will help you hire the right employee the first time, even if you don't adopt this philosophy.

The ads I used to hire the best people described the job briefly and led them to a video where the potential employee could watch in detail what was expected of them, if they applied for this job.

During the video, I showed the training program they would be going through along with some information about each module, and what they would be doing on a day-to-day basis. My videos were only about ten minutes each and at the end I asked them to email me personally and tell me why it was their dream job.

I used the word "dream job" in an assumptive tone, (using the priming technique once again) because working from home is truly a privilege and I wanted someone who was passionate about premium beauty products and health education, which Healthy Revelations was moving more towards at the time.

The result of these types of ads allowed me to hire the right person the first time. If you choose to try this approach yourself, you'll also see how easy it is to hire the perfect person the first time too.

For example, the person you will want to hire for your company will write at least five paragraphs telling you why it's their dream to work for your company. You can expect to hear detailed reasons as to why they are qualified and would love to be a part of your organization.

Assuming the references check out, nine times out of ten you'll find an employee who will be loyal, qualified, and happy to be apart of your organization for years to come.

After I hired the right employee, I created a manager account in the software so each department head could become a manager and train the new employee using the program I had created.

From there, I stood back and watched what happened next.

I gave my newly appointed managers very little instruction other than don't move them onto each module until you are 100% certain they can do their job the way it's required in the training.

Since I was the expert who created the program, I had access to the control panel and watched each employee move through the training. It felt so good to see helpful interaction between each manager and their new employees.

I witnessed several occasions where my manager would ask the employee to do the work again and prove competence. For example, if the email replies to customers did not seem genuine enough, specific parts of the reply would be pasted in the conversation part of the software and corrected by the manager so the employee could see where they went wrong.

From there, the employee was asked to answer more emails and prove competence once again. I loved how my managers

did not simply move the new employee onto the next training module until they really got it. They knew they were accountable and that's why they took their new role as manager so seriously.

Other times, I saw my managers manually graduate employees and give positive comments to reinforce their new found skill.

After hiring enough employees to keep us going, I took a hard look at the programs I created, and realized I had left certain parts out. For example, I forgot to add a lesson that showed the employee how to login to our phone system and switch the phones at the designated time they would be working.

This put all the pressure on my manager to always be the one adjusting the phones. When I realized this error, I quickly added a lesson and video to show new employees how to do this. I then requested they complete one more lesson and that solved the problem.

As another example, I realized that my printed phone script alone was not good enough, because the sales percentage of my new phone reps was much lower than I expected.

So I went back into that specific lesson where the written instruction was, and added a video of me showing the script on screen and reading the script word for word. I explained how to speak with customers in a warm friendly tone and what voice inflections to use and even when to use them.

I also framed the reality that each customer would not be calling unless they were seriously interested in ordering over the phone.

I then had each employee log back into training and go back to the lesson they already completed. They were instructed

to watch my new video and write back telling me what part of the video they found helpful.

Even though my manager was still communicating with the new employee directly, I was able to get feedback that proved my edit helped our new phone rep feel more comfortable on the phone and convert more sales.

One of my phone reps commented that they thought I wanted them to hard sell the potential customers. In the video I created, I conversationally explained a situation where I did not think our products would benefit a particular person.

This was not in the script, but was clearly important. It came out in my video and that helped my reps to have more fun and not feel pressure to over sell.

Looking back on this experience, my software worked perfectly and I couldn't believe how easy it was for my managers to pick it up and train new employees to do their jobs as I mandated. I felt free from my company for the first time in a decade.

The ETC software I spent years developing has proven itself to be a true asset in the success of my Healthy Revelation's company. I believe all companies can benefit from having results focused accountability systems as part of their training programs.

Is your company open to new ideas?

Chapter 16

EVOLVE YOUR JOB TRAINING PROGRAMS NOW OR ALL HECK COULD BREAK LOOSE IN YOUR COMPANY

I'll never forget sitting next to a friendly women named Sarah, who was flying to Las Vegas with me to claim a dog from a breeder while I was on my way to a conference. After getting to know her through friendly conversation, she told me how she was quitting her job, because managing so many people had become too stressful for her.

Sarah worked for a health care company out of Colorado Springs. She told me how the company has continued to grow and that she spent all of her time training new employees and managing existing workers.

Sarah used the phrase "spinning plates" when it came to training and overseeing the details each employee was

responsible for. It was a Saturday morning when we were flying out and she gave her two-week notice the day before.

She now had a new job lined up and was excited to get out of management after being stressed out for so long. I was intrigued to learn more about her current situation and asked her how the company planned on training someone else to take over her position.

Her answer stunned me. Sarah explained that without her managing and overseeing each employee, the company would fall apart. I could tell by the way she said it, that she really meant it.

I asked her how she could help with the transition and Sarah replied by shaking her head back and forth. She explained that even "if" she wrote out details for each worker, there was no way they would be followed unless someone was overseeing their work on a continuous basis.

She felt horrible for leaving the company because she believed that the company would go out of business without her. I began telling her about my ETC software (at the time it was in beta mode) and as I explained how the software worked, her eyes widened.

After a few minutes of explaining my software and helping her understand how she could leave that company with a complete training program in place so a new manager could take over, she took my contact information and told me that she would recommend that the owner take a look at my solution.

I never heard back from Sarah or the owner of that company, which was sort of surprising. Either way, that conversation has always stuck with me. I was amazed that a company who

employed more than twenty people didn't have a training program set up, let alone the fact that they were reliant on one person to train and oversee such a large staff.

For weeks, I just couldn't get Sarah's story out of my mind, and it made me wonder how many other companies didn't have training programs in place. This motivated me to go out of my way and interview friends and acquaintances who ran successful companies.

Luckily for me, I had quite a Rolodex of high-level business owners I have gotten to know over the years. I used my connections to set up meetings and asked each business owner about their current training methods.

What I learned was shocking. Most companies hired new helpers as they grew. They left the training up to current employees and allowed them to become managers. Then the new managers would train their helpers without getting any real feedback.

In terms of how they trained their new employees, some trained face to face, but those companies who used virtual training methods relied on "GoToMeeting". The rest of the virtual training was done through email and phone calls.

About one third of the business owners I spoke with had written procedures documented for each position within their company. Of that one third, only a small portion had updated those procedures within the past year.

For the businesses that had some form of documented procedures, they stored those procedures online (using Google drive mostly) and allowed employees to view those documents as instructed.

Another small portion of the businesses had procedures, recorded training videos and uploaded them to a private YouTube channel. Once they gave employees access, those employees could view the training videos.

The stunning part is that the other two thirds did *not* have any documentation. They simply allowed their employees to do their best work based on upper management's personal instruction.

The majority of the business owners I spoke with did not have adequate training systems in place and after speaking with each, they recognized that was an area they could, and should, improve upon.

Most business owners I spoke with were grateful that I intervened when I did. During several of our conversations, the "what if" scenario came up with the thought that a key employee could leave and what affects that loss would have on their company.

As a disclaimer, I did not speak with any CEO whose company was earning over $10,000,000 per year in revenue. I would think that the larger companies do have better training programs in place, but it does make me wonder.

I also read an article on page 68 of the March, 2014 Inc. Magazine edition that spoke about a research study of more than 100,000 midsize businesses that were self-sustained growth champions measured by how many people they hired from 2007–2012. Fewer than 1.5% of all companies even made the cut to be included in this exclusive survey.

Of this small but mighty group, they asked what potential disaster is of the <u>most</u> concern. 61% of the respondents

reported, "a sudden loss of a key employee". This was the highest percentage among 11 unplanned events that were rated in this survey.

This is a shocking statistic that proves most companies do not have procedures in place let alone a training program to train a new employee if a key employee goes down.

If you feel stuck and unsure how to identify and list your employee job procedures, go to → www.TutorFi.com/procedure-cheat-sheet.

As for me personally, I have seen how my simple software allowed managers and new employees to work in perfect harmony while making sure the details of each job are being trained the way I the expert (Note: I use the word expert to define the creator of each job training program. This is the way it's set up in the software) required in each training program.

Since implementing my training programs, my entire team has appreciated the simplicity of the program and it has allowed me to have more peace of mind than ever before.

As a bonus, I also found that by re-training my current employees, I helped them get more on track with details that have a direct effect on cash flow and the bottom line.

As I work with new businesses and help them set up their own training programs, I expect to see each company achieve the same type of successful outcome.

Chapter 17

IT TAKES GUTS TO EVOLVE THIS WAY, BUT THE PAYOFF IS HUGE

I n Perry Marshall's book called the *80/20 Sales And Marketing*, he speaks about offering a Power Guarantee and why it can propel your company to the top of any industry, if you have the guts to implement it.

Whether you are an expert/coach helping people achieve "X" or a trainer in charge of creating training programs with specific procedures for your company, breakthroughs can happen if you are committed to the end result.

So what is the end result? The achievement of your goal!

If you are an expert in any field, you can guarantee results for your clients.

If you are a trainer for a company, you can guarantee specific results and watch as your employees follow each

74

procedure and achieve each training program goal exactly as you desire.

This thought is probably scarier to trainers than it is to experts who already have their success steps laid out.

If you train in a corporate environment, you would need to be committed to this type of success and become accountable no matter what. This is the type of attitude you must have to make your training programs successful in the long run.

If you don't think it is possible to be accountable for other employees, allow this to be your man in the mirror gut check (as my football coach used to say). I know it sounds crazy to take that much responsibility, but once you master the idea itself, you'll be on your way to success that can only be defined as well beyond your wildest imagination.

The world is changing rapidly. More and more information will be free including online college courses offered by Harvard, Cornell, Davidson and other top educational institutions. A University education like this normally costs thousands of dollars.

So why are these Ivy League universities giving away their online classes for free?

NY Times says, "M.I.T. and Harvard officials said they would use the new online platform not just to build a global community of online learners, but also to research teaching methods and technologies."

"What faculty don't want to do is just take something off the shelf that's somebody else's and teach it, any more than they would take a textbook, start on Page 1, and end with the last chapter," he said. "What's still missing is an online platform

that gives faculty the capacity to customize the content of their own highly interactive courses." http://www.nytimes.com/2012/05/03/education/harvard-and-mit-team-up-to-offer-free-online-courses.html?_r=0

The truth is, they know that automated learning without human interaction has no real value other than to the learner who might be motivated enough on their own to learn and take action. This mostly happens with people living outside of the US. They are truly grateful that our US Universities are offering their course materials for free.

When you add an instructor or professor into the mix, now you have accountability, which equals value. Without real human interaction, it's just helpful information.

If you are a corporate trainer, the value you can provide to your company by adding procedures and internal accountability processes will pay you very well.

If you are an expert (author, speaker, consultant or coach) who can promise a specific result to your client, you just created a new highly priced offer that you did not have before.

This is a true win/win situation. Your employee will be accountable for doing their job as your training program instructs. You'll reduce the stress of your employee's training process, and maintain a happier employee who will feel good knowing that they are doing an excellent job for your company.

The manager you put in place will be responsible for moving each employee through each training module as they prove competence.

If they don't prove competence, they will stay in that specific training module until they do. If the manager keeps running

into sticky points where an employee keeps getting stuck, he or she should report it to the head trainer (expert) who created the procedures and program.

In a situation like this, the head trainer will examine that particular module to see if there is a better way they can present the training material for that particular job.

For a client who is paying for a program from an expert that promises a specific result, the client will be accountable for completing each success step. If they don't complete those success steps to the coaches' satisfaction (you the expert can choose to put coaches in charge of teaching your material), they will not be permitted to move on to the next success step.

If they quit or stop moving forward, they can't expect the promised result, because that result is only promised upon graduation of the program. And again if clients continue to get stuck on one particular success step, the expert must re-examine that lesson and make sure his or her information is being delivered the best way possible.

Now that you have a better understanding of this evolutionary way of training and coaching for a specific result, ask yourself if you are striving for excellence, or just playing it safe?

What's the worst that can happen if you go for it?

In a corporate training environment, the worse that can happen is still better than not having a training and procedural system in place. You will adjust once you get feedback from your employees and that's a good thing! You'll always be improving.

For experts promising a result, it will force you to nail down the lessons and details it will take to guarantee your promised

result. If the client does not do the work, they can't get upset with you and are forced to be accountable.

Once you receive feedback from clients actively moving through your program, you'll instinctively want to make your program better and better.

By simply striving for excellence, both experts and trainers will be the best they can be.

Future opportunities in today's age do and will continue to revolve around accountability along with a personalized & automated (mash up) approach. If you have the guts to put this type of training or coaching program in place, it can pay off in a big way.

Chapter 18

How To Take
Evolutionary
Action

Congratulations on reading this entire book! At this point, you are probably receptive to the idea of creating your own results focused accountability training program and that's great news.

The #1 secret you need to know before creating your own program is, video creation. In most cases, the video instruction you need to thoroughly master will revolve around screen capture video and not directly speaking into your video camera.

Once you get behind this idea, the types of training you can implement are limitless. Here are some examples and specific ways you can and should start to use screen capture videos to help leverage your business.

- Sales script training—show the script and read it as if you were speaking to a potential customer/client. Lead your employee through every possible scenario and make sure your script reflects those possibilities.
- Client training—show your clients exactly how to complete a task that can help them achieve their goals…marketing, seo, programming and anything "how to" related.
- Customer service training—identify types of incoming calls and review the outline script of how to speak to each customer.
- Specific physical task training—for these types of videos, you could show assembly line production, shipping instructions, hotel cleaning and more. Just point the video camera and instruct how you want each job to be done. By having your employees watch how to do the tasks before they do it, they'll be primed perfectly to do the job right the first time.
- How to work efficiently regarding training—by mastering video creation, you can do your work in less time and outsource quickly and easily. The ideas are unlimited: Graphics review with artist, programming review with programmer, quick instructions for employees showing how to methods, hiring videos showing the job you are hiring for and marketing specifics details. Just label each video and you are done.
- And more…

The best screen shot video software I know of is Camtasia, but if you google that term, you can choose from others as well. I like Camtasia, because it lets me instantly upload my video to YouTube.

For a free video on how to create screen shot videos, go to www.TutorFi.com/screen-shot-video

Now that you know the secret of putting together these types of training programs, in this final chapter, you'll discover a handful of the software options you can choose from. Once you have your platform, you simply upload your videos, ask the right questions (or require tasks to be completed) and create your own results focused accountability training program.

First, I have a story to share.

There was a ship traveling from San Francisco to San Diego and back. After the ship docked and delivered its goods, it attempted to start up the engines to return to San Francisco, but the engines would not start.

The mechanic on board spent twenty-seven hours trying to fix the broken ship, but was unable to fix it. He just couldn't figure out where the breakdown occurred.

After forty-eight hours of being stuck at the doc, they hired an outside mechanic who charged $20,000 to fix the problem.

When the mechanic arrived at the broken down ship, he was taken into the bowel of the boat. With a few turns of a screw and a new belt replacement, he was able to fix the broken down engines with only one hour of real work.

He was paid the agreed upon price of $20,000 and left the boat with a smile on his face. In the eyes of the captain, he overpaid for the services of the mechanic, and was mad!

"Who gets paid $20,000 per hour?" the captain said to his crew. One of the deck hands replied back, "The person who knows which screw to turn in order to fix the problem".

This is the lesson I want to pass onto you. It's real easy to be oooohhed and aaaahhed into thinking one of these solutions below can help you, but if you don't know which screw to turn to help your business grow, it won't matter one bit which robust software you choose.

It's my belief that the outside expert mechanic (consultant) should come with your software. If not, it will be difficult for you to set up your program properly and impossible for you to know what areas of your training and coaching program need improved upon.

The software company you choose should have your best interest in mind. You should expect their support staff to check in with you to review your client or employee experience as they progress through each training program you create.

Below is a list of different platforms that can help you create your own online training or coaching program.

http://www.adobe.com/resources/elearning/
http://www.mindflash.com/welcome
http://www.conductit.com/
http://elogiclearning.com/
http://smarteru.com/en/default.cfm
http://www.dojolearning.com

Of course you have the option of using my very own ETC Software too. The main difference between what I offer and what they offer is the fact that we offer a personalized approach

with our clients, because we want to make sure you are getting the absolute most benefits from the programs you create.

Our commitment to your success is very unique. First, my ETC software is only offered to those companies and experts who are in a position to hit the ground running.

If we don't feel you are ready, we'll tell you. In fact, my team does not allow anyone to sign up unless we speak with them first.

The next important thing we do to ensure you hit the ground running is to help you get set up. We do the work for you!

Once we upload your first training program, we schedule a time to review the program and decide on which questions or completed tasks to require, in order to move from one lesson/module to the next.

Then, after your program is up and running, we analyze your program and provide you video feedback (without you even asking) on ways you can improve it. From there, you can decide if you wish to implement the changes or have my team continue to help you implement those changes.

And finally, ongoing consultations are always available for all ETC clients. Sometimes you can't see the obvious fixes because you are so entrenched in the day-to-day operations. My team of certified consultants have been trained to identify multiple methods in which your program can be tweaked to improve the results you wish to focus on.

You can also expect each certified TutorFi ETC consultant to over deliver in ways that are not mentioned above. We are

truly here to help you succeed and do not want one penny from you unless we can do just that.

For more information on our ETC software solutions for experts and companies, go to the links below and schedule your first consultation today.

Experts go to → www.ETCSoftwareSolutions.com/Experts

Corporate trainers go to → www.ETCSoftwareSolutions. com/Trainers

Thanks so much for reading my book. I hope it helped you identify multiple ways you can explode your company.

If you wish to contact me directly, email <u>Scott@TutorFi. com</u>.

Sincerely,

Scott Palat

TutorFi CEO

CPSIA information can be obtained at www.ICGtesting.com
Printed in the USA
BVOW05*2216150315

391764BV00012B/195/P

9 781630 472481